Modern Expressions for Piano

Early Advanced

edited by Helen Marlais

THE FJH
CONTEMPORARY
KEYBOARD
EDITIONS

Valerie Roth Roubos

D1571676

Notes from the Composer

Throughout *Modern Expressions for Piano*, I added a few contemporary twists to each piece. A mix of contemporary and traditional harmonies will transport you to the English seashore in *Rachael by the Sea*. *Berceuse* combines crunchy seconds along with the soothing sounds of a conventional lullaby. At first glance, *Coronation March* seems like a traditional march, but notice the time signature of 5/4. *Elegy* was created as a fond remembrance of loved ones and moves from a minor to a major key. Dissonant intervals are paired with the swaying rhythms of the Caribbean in *Contradanza* for a musical journey to the islands. *Flowers in the Breeze* sway back and forth as the piece alternates from white to black keys. Listen for where the train nearly crashes and then slowly grinds its way back to the top in *Devil's Canyon Railway*.

I hope you enjoy these musical journeys with a modern splash!

Sincerely,
Valerie Roth Roubos

Production: Frank J. Hackinson
Production Coordinators: Peggy Gallagher and Philip Groeber
Cover: Terpstra Design, San Francisco
Cover Painting: *Composition IX*, by Wassily Kandinsky, 1936
Engraving: Tempo Music Press, Inc.
Printer: Tempo Music Press, Inc.

ISBN-13: 978-1-56939-916-3

Copyright © MMXV by
THE FJH MUSIC COMPANY INC. (ASCAP).
2525 Davie Road, Suite 360
Fort Lauderdale, FL 33317-7424
International Copyright Secured.
All Rights Reserved. Printed in U.S.A.

THE
F·J·H
MUSIC
COMPANY
INC.
Frank J. Hackinson

About the Editor

Dr. Marlais is one of the most prolific authors in the field of educational piano music and an exclusive writer for The FJH Music Company Inc. The critically acclaimed and award-winning piano series: *Succeeding at the Piano®* –*A Method for Everyone, Succeeding with the Masters®, The Festival Collection®, In Recital®, Sight Reading and Rhythm Every Day®, Write, Play, and Hear Your Theory Every Day®,* and *The FJH Contemporary Keyboard Editions,* among others, included in The FJH Pianist's Curriculum® by Helen Marlais, are designed to guide students from the beginner through advanced levels. Dr. Marlais gives pedagogical workshops worldwide and the method *Succeeding at the Piano®* is published in South Korea and Taiwan. She presents showcases for The FJH Music Company at national conventions and internationally.

Dr. Marlais has performed and presented throughout the U.S. and in Canada, Italy, England, France, Hungary, Turkey, Germany, Lithuania, Estonia, Australia, New Zealand, China, South Korea, Taiwan, Jamaica, and Russia. She has recorded on Gasparo, Centaur and Audite record labels with her husband, concert clarinetist Arthur Campbell. Their recording, *Music for Clarinet and Piano,* was nominated for the 2013 *International Classical Music Awards,* one of the most prestigious distinctions available to classical musicians today. She has also recorded numerous educational piano CD's for Stargrass Records®. She has performed with members of the Chicago, Pittsburgh, Minnesota, Grand Rapids, Des Moines, Cedar Rapids, and Beijing National Symphony Orchestras, and has premiered many new works by contemporary composers from the United States, Canada, and Europe. Dr. Marlais received her DM in piano performance and pedagogy from Northwestern University, her MFA in piano performance from Carnegie Mellon University, and was awarded the Outstanding Alumna in the Arts from the University of Toledo, where she received her bachelor of music degree in piano performance. As well as being the Director of Keyboard Publications for The FJH Music Company, Dr. Marlais is also an Associate Professor of Music at Grand Valley State University in Grand Rapids, Michigan. Visit: www.helenmarlais.com

A Special Note to Students

Welcome to the exciting world of music written for you during our time! The composer of this collection is someone you could actually speak to and meet! You will discover new sounds and pedal effects, and interesting melodies, rhythms, and harmonies that will be fun to play! You will notice that the pieces in this collection are contrasting in nature—some are energetic, others lyrical—some are sad, others are humorous.

As you explore this book, use your imagination to create your very own interpretation of these wonderful new pieces. The title of each work will give you your first clue as to how to bring the piece to life, and the musical indications (tempo, dynamics, articulation and pedal markings, etc.) will provide a map to guide you through this exciting musical journey.

Enjoy these pieces!

Sincerely,
Helen Marlais

About the Composer

Valerie Roth Roubos earned degrees in music theory and composition and flute performance from the University of Wyoming. Ms. Roubos maintains a studio in her home in Spokane, Washington, where she teaches flute, piano, and composition. Valerie also enjoys playing autoharp, flute, and pennywhistle in a bluegrass band. Valerie's teaching philosophy and compositions reflect her belief that all students, from elementary to advanced, are capable of musical playing that incorporates sensitivity and expression. Ms. Roubos' choral and piano works represent a variety of musical styles including sacred and secular. In 2001, the South Dakota Music Teachers Association selected Ms. Roubos as Composer of the Year. Valerie was chosen to be the 2004-2005 composer-in-residence at Washington State University. In 2006, the Washington State Music Teachers Association named her Composer of the Year. The Wyoming Music Teachers Association selected her as the Composer of the Year for 2007. Washington State University selected Valerie as the Adopted Composer for 2009-2010.

Active as a performer, adjudicator, lecturer, and accompanist, Ms. Roubos has lectured at the Washington State Music Teachers Conference. She has presented workshops at Holy Names Music Center, Spokane Music Teachers Association, Tri-Cities Music Teachers Association, Lake Washington Music Teachers Association, and the Clark County Music Teachers Association. In 2011, the Wenatchee Valley Music Teachers Association selected Valerie to compose a piece for the dedication recital of the chapter's new piano. She has served as the chair of the WSMTA Composer Commissioning Committee and has played an active role in the Spokane Music Teachers Association. For the 25th anniversary in 2012, Holy Names Music Center selected Valerie as the featured composer.

Table of Contents

Rachael by the Sea

Valerie Roth Roubos

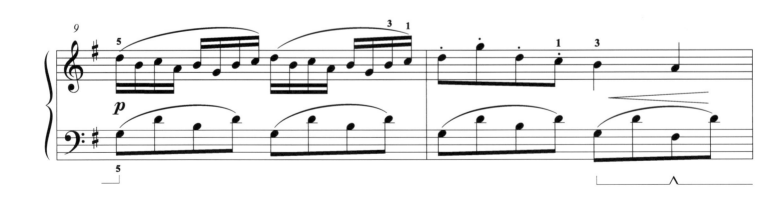

4

Meno mosso

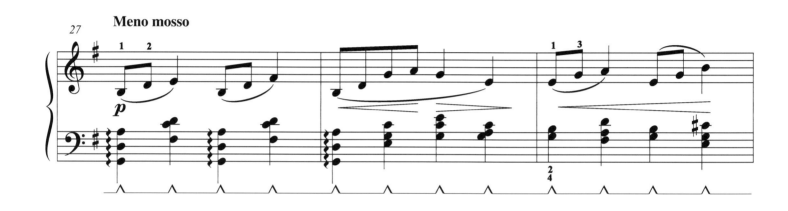

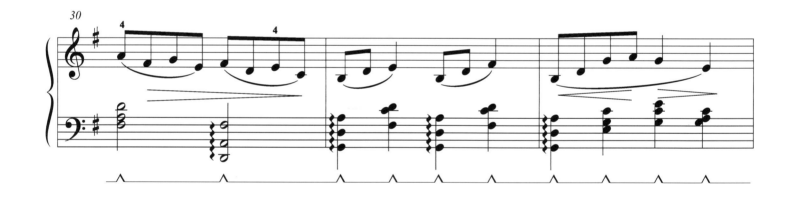

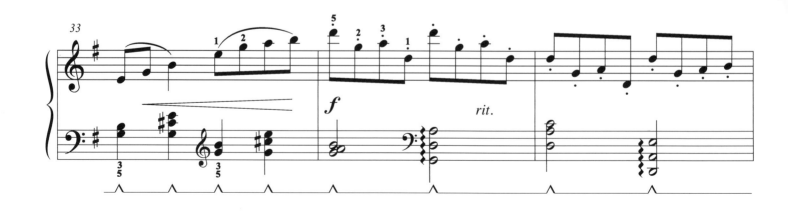

Berceuse

Valerie Roth Roubos

Andante moderato (♩. = ca. 56)

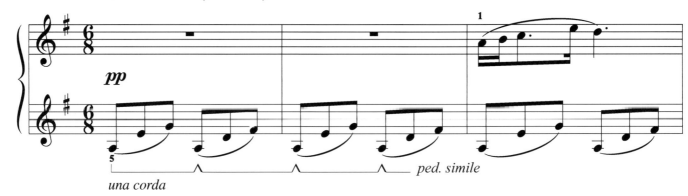

pp

una corda

ped. simile

p

tre corde

poco rit.

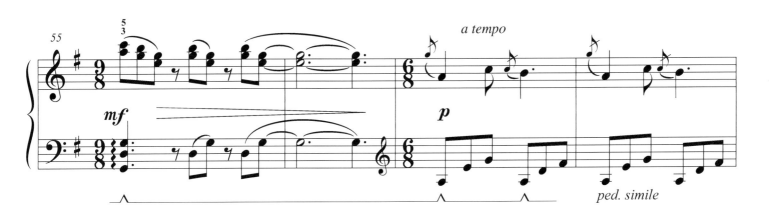

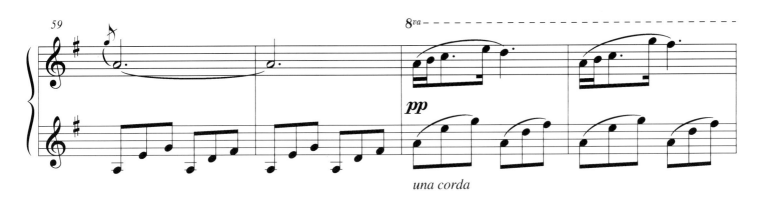

Coronation March

Valerie Roth Roubos

Maestoso (♩ = ca. 104)

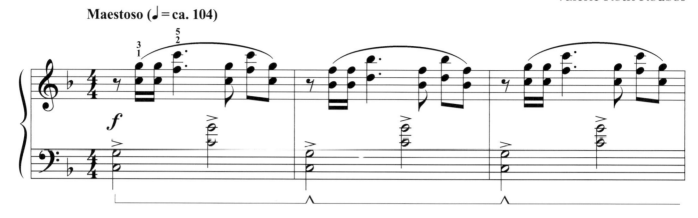

14

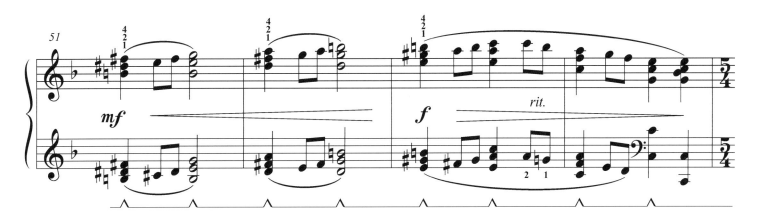

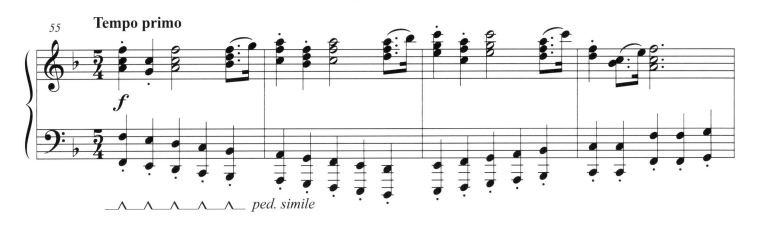

Elegy

Valerie Roth Roubos

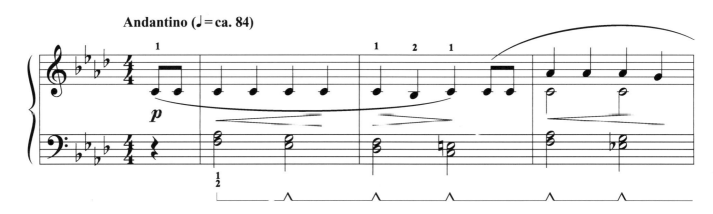

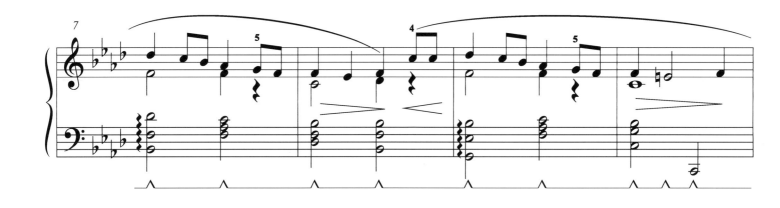

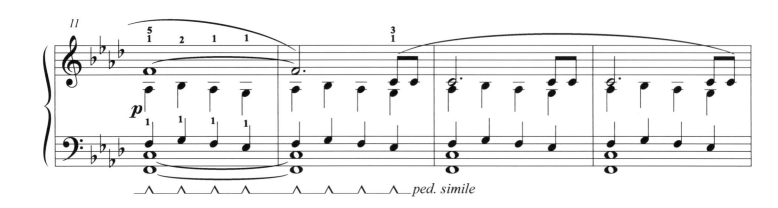

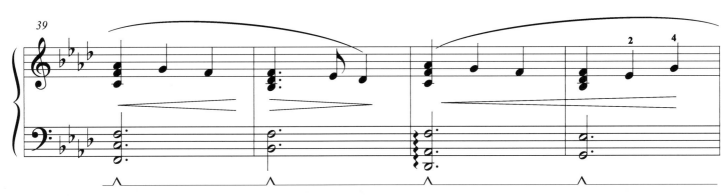

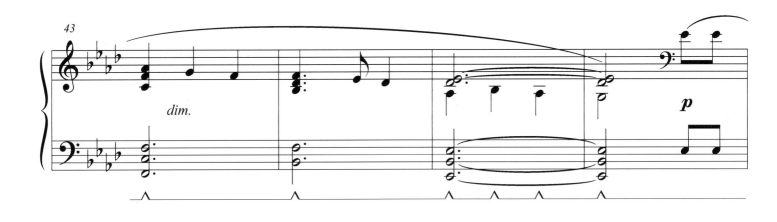

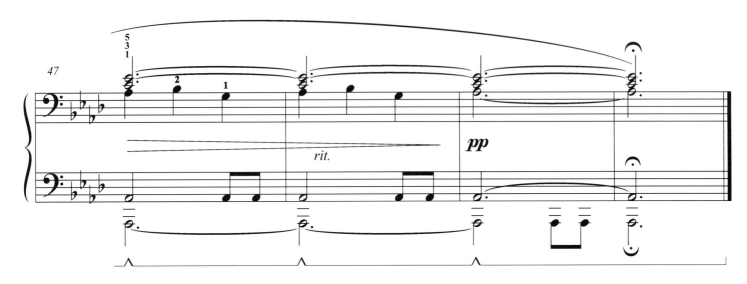

Contradanza

Valerie Roth Roubos

J1030

Flowers in the Breeze

Valerie Roth Roubos

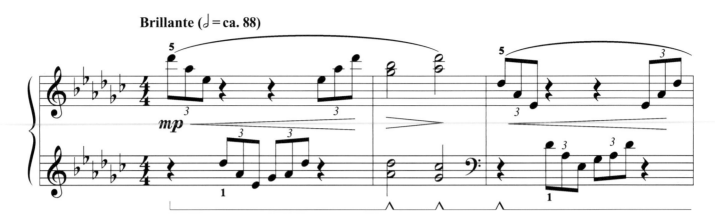

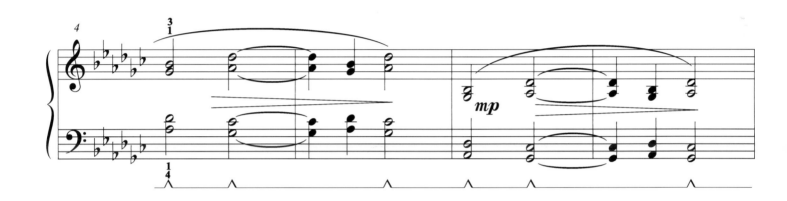

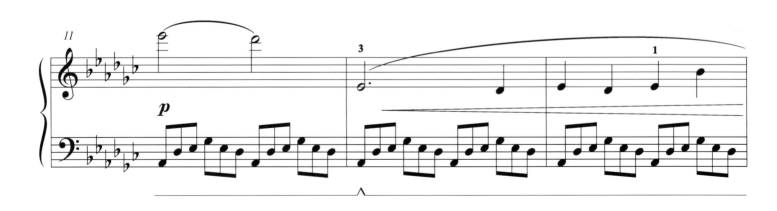

24

26

J1030

Devil's Canyon Railway

Valerie Roth Roubos

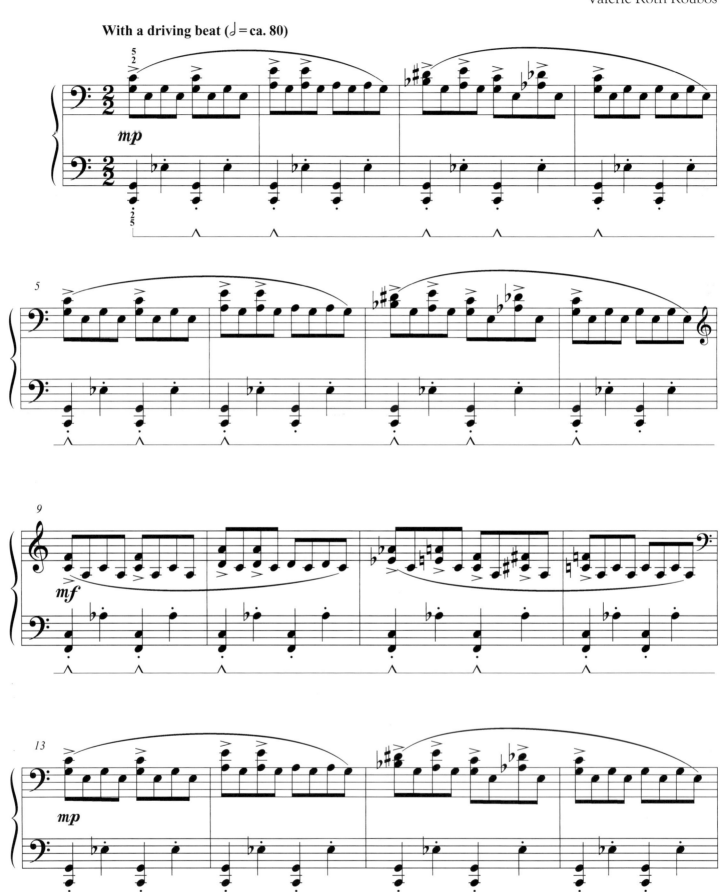

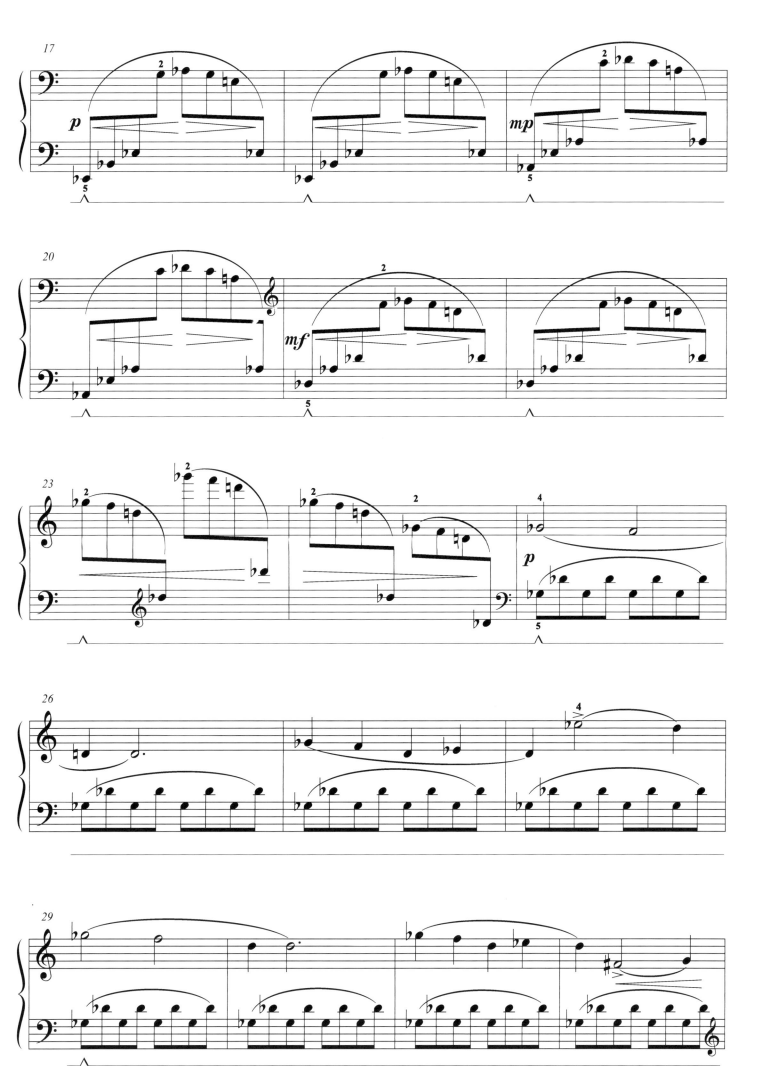

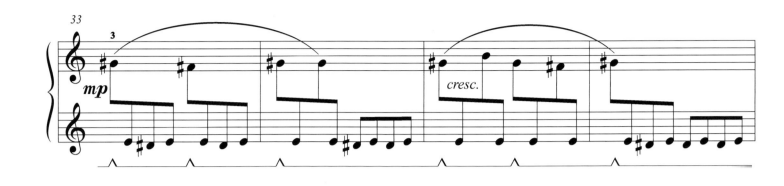

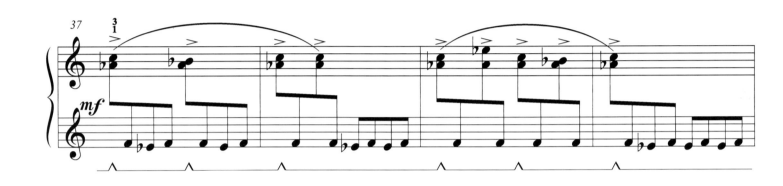

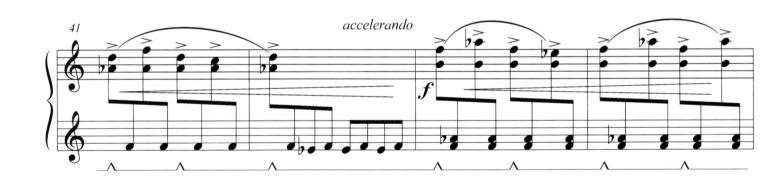

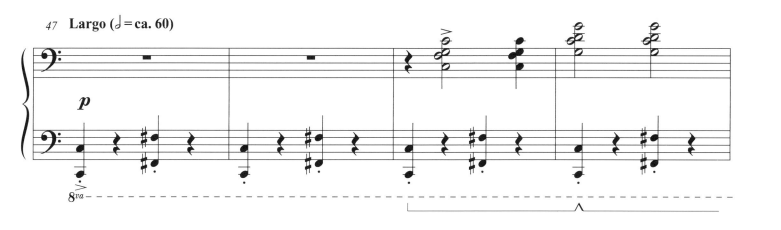

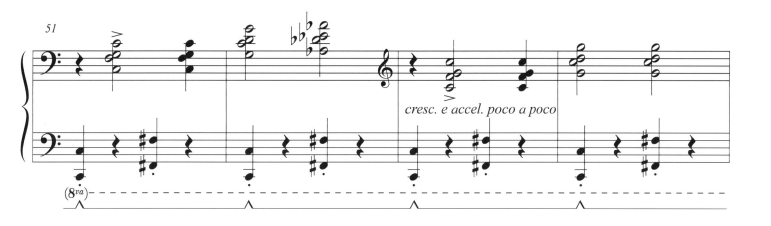

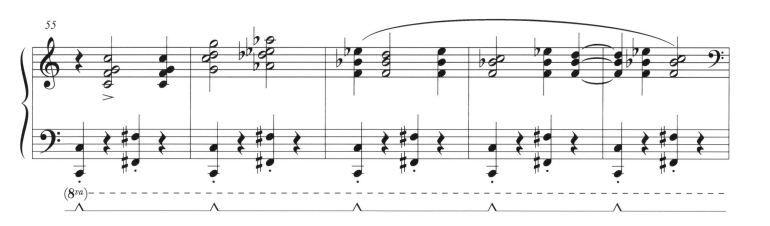

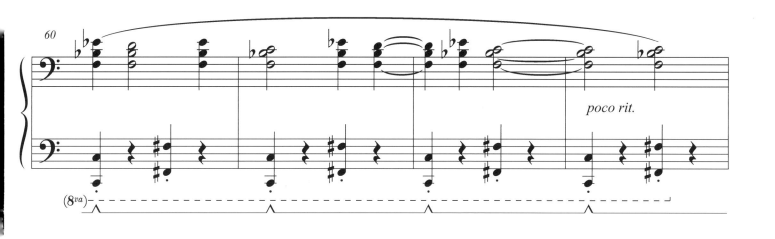

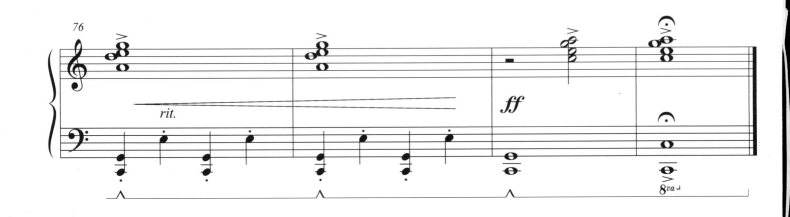